Who Is My Mom?

By Melissa Nicholas
Illustrated by Jean Cassels

Sadlier-Oxford
A Division of William H. Sadlier, Inc.

2 My mom is a mouse.

My mom is a chipmunk.

3

My mom is a moose.

My mom is a bear.

6 My mom is a monkey.

My mom is a penguin.

8 Who is my mom?